The Varangian Guard: The History and Legacy of the Byzantine Empire's Elite Mercenary Unit

By Charles River Editors

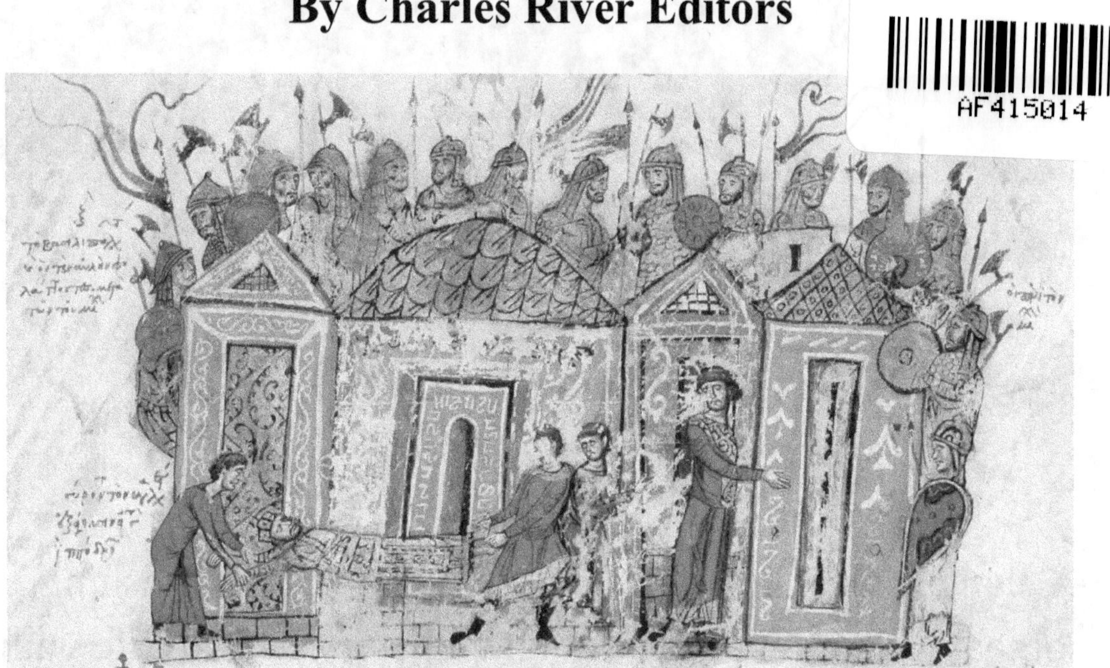

A medieval depiction of the Varangian Guard

About Charles River Editors

Charles River Editors is a boutique digital publishing company, specializing in bringing history back to life with educational and engaging books on a wide range of topics. Keep up to date with our new and free offerings with this 5 second sign up on our weekly mailing list, and visit Our Kindle Author Page to see other recently published Kindle titles.

We make these books for you and always want to know our readers' opinions, so we encourage you to leave reviews and look forward to publishing new and exciting titles each week.

Introduction

The seal of the Varangian Guard's Grand Interpreter

The Byzantine Empire was the heir to two great cultures that cradled and nurtured European civilization: Greece and Rome. Constantinople, now called Istanbul, became a center of power, culture, trade, and technology poised on the edges of Europe and Asia, and its influence was felt not only throughout Europe but the Middle East, Africa, Central Asia, and the Far East. Coins dating from the reign of Emperor Justinian I (r.527-565) have been found in southern India, and Chinese records show that the "Fulin," as the Chinese named the Byzantines, were received at court as early as 643 CE. For a thousand years, the Byzantine Empire protected Europe from the Islamic Arab Empire, allowing it to pursue its own destiny. Finally, Byzantium was a polyglot society in which a multitude of ethnic groups lived under the emperor prizing peace above war, an inspiration surely for the modern age when divisive nationalism threatens to dominate society once more.

In terms of geopolitics, perhaps the most seminal event of the Middle Ages was the successful Ottoman siege of Constantinople in 1453. The city had been an imperial capital as far back as the 4th century, when Constantine the Great shifted the power center of the Roman Empire there, effectively establishing two almost equally powerful halves of antiquity's greatest empire. Constantinople would continue to serve as the capital of the Byzantine Empire even after the Western half of the Roman Empire collapsed in the late 5th century. Naturally, the Ottoman Empire would also use Constantinople as the capital of its empire after their conquest effectively ended the Byzantine Empire, and thanks to its strategic location, it has been a trading center for years and remains one today under the Turkish name of Istanbul.

The Ottoman conquest of Constantinople also played a decisive role in fostering the Renaissance in Western Europe. The Byzantine Empire's influence had helped ensure that it was the custodian of various ancient texts, most notably from the ancient Greeks, and when Constantinople fell, Byzantine refugees flocked west to seek refuge in Europe. Those refugees brought books that helped spark an interest in antiquity that fueled the Italian Renaissance and essentially put an end to the Middle Ages altogether. This was why, in November 2004, French President Jacques Chirac addressed a student conference in Marseilles and explained why the Republic of Turkey was joining the European Union. In response to protests that Turkey did not share European culture and values, especially when the Ottoman Empire in centuries past sought to destroy Europe, Chirac pointed out that Turkey was the cultural heir of the Byzantine Empire, and that "we are all the children of Byzantium."

Despite all this, the Byzantine Empire is often treated as a medieval oddity, an absolute state stunted by a myopic religion, a corrupt, labyrinthine bureaucracy, and an inability to adapt to change. In truth, none of these judgments bear any serious scrutiny - Byzantium was a strong, organized, highly effective and adaptable civilization for most of its long history. It owed its success in no small part to its military, which, in contrast to the feudal armies of Western Europe and the tribally based forces of the Middle East, operated with a high level of discipline, strategic prowess, efficiency, and organization.

At the same time, the Byzantines relied heavily on mercenaries, and the *Hetairoi* or foreign soldiers formed an important and often vital component of the army. The ability to call upon warriors from many nations demonstrated the power and wealth of the emperor, so they were recruited as much for prestige as for military utility.

The most famous of the foreign units was without question the Varangian Guard. The Varangians came from the land in Eastern Europe known in the Middle Ages as Rus, which is now part of modern Russia and Ukraine. They were descendants of Viking warriors from Sweden who came to rule the waterways and population of Russia. Varangian mercenaries were fighting for the Byzantines by the 10th century, and in 988 they formed a permanent elite guard for the emperor. They took an oath of allegiance to him and served directly under the Acolyte or *Akolouthos*, who was usually of Byzantine origin. They also assumed responsibilities for the security of Constantinople. They served in battles outside the capital, but usually only when necessity called for it.

The Varangian Guard's primary duty was always to protect the emperor, and inevitably, the Varangians became a political force, taking part in the numerous palace coups. They displayed a fierce devotion not necessarily to the emperor but to the throne itself - for example, when Emperor Nicephorus II was murdered by John I Tzimiskes in 969, the Varangian Guard immediately pledged its allegiance to the usurper.[1]

---

[1] Norwich, John J., *A Short History of Byzantium*, Viking, 1997

The Guard consisted of heavily armored infantry bearing shields, heavy swords, and Norse battle axes, either single-bladed or double-bladed. They were amongst the fiercest and most feared military units in Christendom, which made the unit an attractive station for many soldiers of fortune came to Constantinople hoping to pursue lucrative military careers in the service of the Byzantine emperors. Those from the West were called at various times *Frankoi*, (Franks),[2] *Latinoi* (Latins, i.e. Latin Rite Christians), or Normans. Frankish knights were often hired to combat the Turks in the 11th century.

The Varangian Guard: The History and Legacy of the Byzantine Empire's Elite Mercenary Unit examines the origins of the emperor's personal bodyguards, and the impact the unit had on Byzantine history. Along with pictures depicting important people, places, and events, you will learn about the Varangian Guard like never before.

---

[2] Frank is a generic term used in the east to refer to Latin Rite Christians.

The Byzantine Empire Before the Varangian Guard

In the ancient world, Rome was a center of learning and culture and the heart of one of the most powerful empires ever created. For around 600 years, the Roman Republic and then the Roman Empire dominated Europe, the Mediterranean and the Middle East and Rome became the most important city in the Western World. However, by the second century, military conquest had slowed and commerce had become far more important. Rome, located far down the Italian peninsula, was not well-placed to become a center of trade and even administration of the massive empire had become challenging.

In 293 CE this problem was formally recognized when Emperor Diocletian created a new administrative system that divided the Roman Empire into eastern and western provinces. The city of Rome was still the heart of the empire and the main city of the Western Province as well as the residence of the Emperor, but the eastern province became more and more significant in terms of trade.

20 years later, Emperor Constantine I became the first Roman ruler to accept Christianity, and the Edict of Milan in 313 declared that Christianity was to be tolerated within the Roman Empire. The Edict of Milan was not quite the landmark that Christian scholars declared it to be, given that Galerius had issued a similar edict shortly before his

death. In Galerius's edict in 311, Christians who "followed such a caprice and had fallen into such a folly that they would not obey the institutes of antiquity" were excused from their "errors": "Wherefore, for this our indulgence, they ought to pray to their God for our safety, for that of the republic, and for their own, that the commonwealth may continue uninjured on every side, and that they may be able to live securely in their homes." With that said, the Edict of Milan certainly went further than Galerius did, by declaring all religions exempt from persecution and proclaiming freedom of worship for all, with a special emphasis on Christianity. Not only were Christians freed from any persecution and allowed to worship in peace, but their property (including entire churches) and wealth that had previously been seized in various religious purges over the years were granted to them with full restitution.

  Constantine took then an even more dramatic step by moving the imperial residence to the ancient Greek city of Byzantium located on the Bosporus, far to the east of Rome. Byzantium was strategically located on the nexus of important trade routes between Europe and Asia and between the Mediterranean and the Black Sea. In 330, the city was renamed Constantinople (the "city of Constantine") and formally declared to be the new capital not just of the eastern province but of the whole Roman Empire.

In Constantinople, the emperor began an unprecedentedly vast program of reconstruction and expansion which was initially named *Nova Roma Constantiniana* ("the new Rome of Constantine"). In a departure from his previously theologically ambivalent religious policies, Constantine chose to erect only Christian temples in his new city, even replacing some older pagan structures, and placed relics in "religiously strategic" places throughout the city to extend divine protection over the walls of what quickly became known colloquially as Constantinople.

Hagia Eirene, the first church commissioned by Constantine in Constantinople

In his time, Constantine affected nearly every conceivable cultural aspect of the Roman Empire, most notably in its religion but also even in attire and appearance. Constantine revived the clean shaven look, which Augustus himself had favored 300 years earlier. Given his conversion of the empire and relocation to Constantinople, Constantine directly shaped the histories of Europe, the Byzantine Empire, the Roman Empire, and the growth of the Catholic Church.

By the late 4th century, Rome had been sacked by invading Goths while Constantinople remained secure, and as the Western Roman Empire suffered, Constantinople became the most powerful city in Europe. The Roman Empire became the predominantly Christian Byzantine Empire. Although the Byzantine Empire grew out of the Roman Empire (and its citizens continued to refer to themselves as Roman), the new empire gradually changed in character. Not only was the new empire Christian, but Greek was the main language used, and by the Middle Ages, Constantinople was the most important and powerful Christian city in Europe.

In 867, a new emperor (*basilieus*) took the throne of the Byzantine Empire. Basil I was an Armenian from a humble background who rose to prominence when he was employed by Theophilitzes, a relative of Emperor Michael III. Basil then inherited wealth and became so influential and powerful that in 866 he was appointed as "Guardian of the Imperial Bedroom" (*parakoimomenos*) by the emperor. One of Basil's tasks was to protect the emperor from those who sought to usurp his power. However, it quickly became clear that the Armenian was ambitious for himself.

Basil quickly came into conflict with the most powerful
general in the empire, Bardas, the emperor's uncle and
chief minister. Bardas was so nervous of Basil that he told
the emperor Basil was a "lion who would devour them
all." To reassure Bardas, the emperor forced Basil to sign
a sacred pact promising that he would not harm the
general. Basil signed the pact and then killed Bardas
anyway, telling the emperor that the general was a traitor.

In 866, Emperor Michael, perhaps nervous of the
growing power of Basil, was forced to make the
Armenian co-emperor, an extraordinary move that had
never been done. Michael announced, "It is my will that
Basil, the High Chamberlain, who is loyal to me, who has
delivered me from my enemy and who holds me in great
affection, should be the guardian and manager of my
Empire and should be proclaimed by all as *basilieus*.[3]"

Basil found himself serving alongside Michael, who was
known as "Michael the Drunkard" for his abiding love of
wine, but Michael attempted to make it clear from the
beginning that Basil was to be his junior. In the same vein,
Michael attempted to limit his power, and in some cases
Michael tried to use Basil to further his own aims. For
example, Michael had a mistress, Eudokia, who was
pregnant, but the Royal Court would not accept her as a
potential queen, so Michael was forced to marry a woman

---

[3] Norwich, J.J. *A Short History of Byzantium*. Vintage, 1998.

from an aristocratic family. However, to keep Eudokia in the royal court, Michael ordered Basil to divorce his wife and marry the emperor's mistress. Basil agreed, though he never shared Eudokia's bed – she continued to be Michael's mistress. To console Basil, Michael had one of his sisters, Thekla, withdraw from the nunnery in which she had been confined. She was ordered to become Basil's mistress.

This arrangement suited Michael, and when Eudokia gave birth to two sons, Leo and Stephen, Basil was officially the children's father, though everyone was aware that their real father was Michael. Michael even intended to appoint Leo as his successor. When Basil was appointed co-emperor, he was also adopted into the royal family, and most people interpreted this as an effort by Michael to make it easier to have Leo appointed as the next emperor.

Basil must also have realized that his own position was precarious, and that he was useful only until Michael was able to establish Leo as his formal heir. In 867, the emperor ominously told Basil, "I made you emperor, and have I not the power to create another emperor if I will?" To counter this, Basil worked hard to gather a group of followers loyal to him, and in September 867, Basil and group of his men burst into the emperor's bedchamber. They found the emperor and some of his principal followers insensibly drunk and promptly killed all of them.

   Despite the fact that he had personally murdered Michael, as co-emperor, Basil automatically became the sole ruler of the Byzantine Empire, and under his autocratic and sometimes brutal rule, the empire would expand dramatically. Basil I was the first of what would become known the Macedonian Dynasty, and that dynasty would rule the Byzantine Empire for over 200 years. No one is quite certain why the dynasty founded by Basil was given this name since he was not a Macedonian, but some historians speculate that he was given the nickname "Macedonian" after spending time in captivity with a number of men from that region after they were captured while fighting Bulgars in the northern territories.

A medieval depiction of Basil and his son Leo holding a sword

Before Basil seized the throne, the empire had been going through a period of slow but steady decline. Islamic attacks in the 7th and 8th centuries had taken the Levant (including the city of Jerusalem) and Byzantine territory in North Africa and Asia. These attacks included two extended sieges of the city of Constantinople, in 674-678 and 717-718, though it was able to withstand both. In the 9th century, attacks by the Bulgars took many of the empire's northern territories and even southern Italy was lost. Thus, when Basil took the throne, his priority was to re-establish the military power of the empire and to take back the lands it had lost under his predecessors.

As the Byzantine Empire's early history demonstrates, the Byzantines were constantly at war, and they would be until Constantinople fell to the Ottoman Turks in 1453. Accordingly, even before the Macedonian Dynasty ushered in the empire's golden age, a great emphasis was placed on the military, which was highly organized, specialized, and methodically maintained, in contrast to the feudal armies of the European west which were only haphazardly raised when needed. The power of the imperial military made it one of the major powers of Europe and the Middle East for the greater part of a millennium.

Drawing upon the legacy both of ancient Greece and Rome, Byzantine scholars composed detailed and comprehensive military manuals with technical precision, so it's somewhat surprising that a culture of warfare for its own sake was utterly alien to Byzantine society. War was generally condemned, even as it was acknowledged to be a necessary evil. The Byzantines did engage in wars of conquest, but it was usually undertaken under the guise of restoring the Roman Empire's integrity, as when Justinian I's forces reconquered Italy, Northern Africa and Southern Spain. For the most part, the imperial military engaged in defensive wars against its numerous enemies.

This ambivalent attitude toward warfare was reflected in the teachings of the Eastern Christian Church, which permeated every aspect of Byzantine society. The Church did recognize that killing might be necessary, but as something to be pardoned rather than blessed. When the Emperor Nicephorus II (r. 963-969) attempted to declare soldiers killed in wars against Muslim invaders martyrs, the bishops replied, "How could they be regarded martyrs or equal to the martyrs, those who kill others or die themselves at war, when the divine canons [ecclesiastical regulations] impose a penalty on them, preventing them from coming to Divine Communion for three years?"[4] Even today, the Patriarch of Constantinople, Bartholomew

---

[4] "Just War: Church and State", Orthodox Wiki, www.orthodoxwiki.org

I, has stated that "in a few specific cases the Orthodox Church forgives an armed defence against oppression and violence."[5]

This attitude is in marked contrast to the theological tradition of the Catholic Church, which gave to rulers the absolute right to go to war to defend their rights and the rights of the Church. This teaching was developed by Thomas Aquinas in the 13th century as the Just War theory,[6] but even before Aquinas, theologians were justifying the Crusades in the Middle East, Spain, and northern Europe, as well as wars to extirpate heretical communities. To the Byzantines, the concept of the holy war as evinced by the Roman Church was repugnant, and they were even more repulsed by the concept of violent jihad upheld as sacred by their Muslim enemies.[7]

When Constantine led the empire, the basic military unit was still the legion, based on the Roman model. Both in the Western Roman Empire and Eastern Roman Empire, the legions would vary greatly in numbers on account of the external pressures brought upon the empire by barbarian incursions. The average size of a legion in this period was roughly 1,000, composed mostly of infantry,

---

[5] Address in Novi Sad (Serbia) October 22 1999

[6] *Summa Theologiae*, II, secunda pars, q. 40

[7] The Arabic word signifies a striving or struggling toward a holy purpose. In Islam it has a variety of meanings, though in historical Islamic law it is most often associated with warfare against non-Muslims. Peters, Rudolph & Cook, David, "Jihad", *The Oxford Encyclopaedia of Islam and Politics*, Oxford University Press 2014

but cavalry were becoming more important and their role was expanding significantly.

The legions were divided into *limitanei*, who garrisoned the *limes* or border forts, and the *comitatenses*, who were stationed in the interior so as to move quickly to where they might be required. The ranks of the legions were heavily supplemented by *foederati*, Germanic tribesmen who were accorded subsidies in return for military service. These subsidies were often in the forms of food or gold, but they were also often given limited settlement rights on Roman soil. The Roman authorities needed to resort to these measures because there was simply not enough tax revenue or manpower to maintain the legions. It has been estimated that Germanics made up as much as a quarter of army officers and lower ranks by the beginning of the 5th century, when the Western Roman Empire was already on the brink.[8]

In addition to the legions and the *foederati*, there were also the *bucellarii*, who were not supported directly by the state. Rather, they were small units raised by individuals such as generals, governors or great landowners. These private soldiers were often better equipped, trained, and paid than state troops. They were often recruited during civil wars and when the state could not or would not

---

[8] Elton, Hugh , *Warfare and the Military, The Cambridge Companion to the Age of Constantine*, Cambridge University Press 2006, pp. 148-149

supply troops to defend the local population. Their name translates as "biscuit-eater," a probable reference to the rations they carried (a *buccellatum* was a hard biscuit of flour, salt and water).

The military's outfits changed markedly in the 4th century as Constantine was shifting his power base east. The short-sleeved and short-skirted tunic of the classical Mediterranean warrior was replaced by clothing more suited to cooler temperatures. Officers wore long-sleeved tunics and trousers often adopting barbarian styles. Tunic and cloaks were often decorated with embroidery or roundels, and soldiers often wore the *pileus pannonicus* or Pannonian cap, a brimless cloth cap not unlike a fez. In battle, they tended to wear chain or mail armor, in contrast to the strip-metal cuirasses worn by earlier Roman soldiers. The helmet and shield remained standard equipment, though the *gladius* or shortsword was phased out in favor of the *spatha*, which was about 760 millimeters long. The composite bow remained a weapon for both infantry and cavalry archers.

During the reign of Emperor Justinian I (r. 527-565), the threat of a Germanic invasion had passed and the most serious threat to the empire was now the Sassanids. To meet the threat, there occurred a gradual reorganization of the military. The ancient legions were abolished, replaced by small infantry or cavalry units. The *numerus* was introduced: a group of 300-400 men. Two or more *numeri* formed a *moira*; two or more *moira*, a *meros*. The four classifications of soldiers, the *comitatenses, limitanei, foederati*, and *bucellarii,* remained. Barbarians no longer dominated the army, and the stabilization of Roman society after the barbarian invasions meant that Roman citizens could freely enlist. The *bucellarii* played a more significant role, notably in the cavalry. They took oaths of loyalty both to the emperor and to the wealthy general, official or nobleman who had hired them.

To this list can be added the *Excubitores,* a class of soldier created by the Emperor Leo I (r.457-474) around the year 460. The name means "those who get out of bed," in other words, sentinels, and they constituted the imperial guard in the capital, Constantinople. They were recruited largely from the Isauria region in southern Asia Minor, a land renowned for its warlike men. The Excubitores were the emperor's elite troops *par excellence* and were entrusted with the safety of the capital and of the imperial person. Their commander, the Count of the Excubitores (*Comes Excubitorum*), was usually a member of the imperial family and one of the most powerful officeholders in the empire.

The military developed heavy armor during this period, largely in response to the Persians. Heavy infantrymen were called "the shielded ones," *skutatoi.* It was in this time that the famous *kataphractoi* developed from the heavy cavalry and came into their own. The name signifies "completely covered," for both rider and horse were heavily armored. The cataphracts constituted the elite of the imperial army. Light cavalry and infantry continued to be used in the Roman army, but with a largely supportive function.

The introduction of the *thema* system came in the 7th century. This radical reorganization of the government and military of the border occurred as a response to the wars with the Islamic Caliphate. The massive losses in Africa and the Middle East greatly reduced the population of the Byzantine Empire and consequently its manpower and revenue. Its remaining territories in Thrace, Asia Minor and southern Italy were divided into *themata*, or themes, and each theme was governed by a *strategos* or general, with a civilian judge or *krites* exercising judicial authority. The origins of this system can be traced to the beginning of the 7th century when the chief general or *magister militum* assumed prominence over the civilian governor. This arrangement overturned 400 years of policy separating the military and government.

In the theme system, the *strategos* divided the land in his theme amongst his soldiers. They remained a military unit and were called for service when required. The *strategos* did not own the land however, as the feudal nobility of

Western Europe did, because the state continued to own the land and granted it to the *strategos* on lease. He taxed the population on behalf of the emperor, keeping a share of the revenue for himself. The soldier-farmers did however possess the right to hand their leases to their descendants, on condition that they also serve in the military. The *strategos* too might pass on his rights and responsibilities to his male children.

The theme system had several advantages, including a reduction in military expenses for the imperial treasury, giving soldiers a vested interest in defending the land in which they lived, a reduction of unpopular conscription, and a means of settling conquered lands. The obvious disadvantage was it that created in the *strategoi* autonomous powers that made it possible for them to rebel against the emperor. To counter this, the imperial government reduced the sizes of the themes and increased their number, particularly after Artabasdos, the *Strategos* of Armenia, usurped the throne briefly in 741.

Another response to the power of the *strategoi* was the augmentation of the imperial guard, which was transformed from a garrison for the city of Constantinople to a standing army. The Excubitor units were expanded into regiments or *tagmata*. These troops were permanently battle-ready and loyal to the emperor alone. In addition to these regiments, the emperor could also call upon the

Hetaireia ("Companions"), a mercenary corps composed of foreign troops. Khazars from the Russian steppes, Magyar, Franks, Varangians (the Vikings who ruled Kiev) and even Arabs often joined these units. By the beginning of the 11th century, it has been estimated that as many as half the troops fighting for the Byzantines were mercenaries, and these men came from all over Europe, including Italians, Franks, Dacians and even a large contingent of Normans. Rather than being integrated into existing units of the army, these foreign mercenaries formed their own units, *symmachoi* (allies), with leaders and officers from the same ethnic background who spoke the same language.

It was from among these mercenary groups that the most unique unit of them all, the Varangian Guard, would rise to the top.

The Origins of the Varangian Guard

Given that he had taken the role of sole emperor by killing Michael and that Basil was illiterate and of humble peasant origins, perhaps the most surprising thing about his rule was that he quickly proved to be an effective and respected emperor. Before beginning his campaign of conquest, Basil I started work on transforming Constantinople into a worthy capital. The city was in a poor state when he took the throne, still recovering from the effects of two long sieges and damage caused by a series of earthquakes. Basil had a magnificent new palace constructed, the *Kainourgion*, and is credited with starting the construction of the sumptuous *Nea Ekklesia* ("New Church") within the grounds of the new royal palace. He also had many public buildings restored and oversaw the reconstruction of the city walls.

Basil ordered a complete overhaul of Byzantine law, intending to make the laws simpler, easier to understand and applicable equally to all. The outcome was the *Basilika* ("Imperial Law"), a suite of new legislation which would remain in force for almost 600 years. He also immediately made himself popular by ending the excesses of Michael's rule, which had seen the Imperial treasury dwindle to almost nothing. Basil curbed spending and even demanded the return of some of the lavish gifts that Michael had bestowed on friends and followers. By doing these things, Basil was able to balance the empire's books without raising taxes, something that made him popular with all levels of Byzantine society.

However, while Basil I was an effective ruler, he was far from benevolent. He had Michael's son Stephen castrated and confined to a monastery. He also planned to have the emperor's other son, Leo, either killed or blinded, and he was only prevented from this by Leo's popularity with the public, as well as opposition from the Church.

Basil I also proved to be an adept military leader. A long-term aim of the empire had been a desire to establish some measure of influence over the Slavic people in the Balkans. Under Basil's rule, the Byzantine Empire gained ecclesiastical control over the emerging Bulgar state, an important step forward. The Byzantine navy also performed well during this period - pirates in the Mediterranean had become a major problem, but under Basil's guidance, they were crushed and Cyprus was retaken from Muslim control.

On land, the armies of the empire performed well. The heretical Paulicians, who lived on the borders of the Armenian province, were defeated in 872 by a Byzantine army commanded by Basil's son-in-law, Christopher. In the southeast of the empire, land was taken from the Emir of Tarsus after the victory of another Byzantine army commanded by Nicephorus Phocas the Elder. In southern Italy, the Byzantine situation was improved though a combination of military campaigns and negotiations with the Frankish Emperor Louis II and the Lombard-controlled duchy of Benevento.

By 886, the Byzantine Empire was larger and more powerful than it had been under any previous emperor, but the question of who would succeed him had come increasingly to trouble Basil. His favored heir was his son from his first marriage, Constantine, but Constantine died in 879, leaving Basil's son by Eudokia, Alexander, as the logical heir. In 879, Basil confirmed this when he appointed the nine-year-old Alexander as co-emperor.

Of course, there was another claimant to the throne: Leo. Leo was still formally named as one of Basil's children, though it was widely accepted that his father had actually been Michael. Basil clearly feared Leo's popularity and had him imprisoned for a short time, possibly intending to have him killed. Intervention by senior members of the church averted this, but Basil was clearly concerned that this "son" might try to attempt to avenge the death of his real father, so he kept Leo as far from power as possible.

In 886, Basil went on one of his frequent hunting expeditions. A stag was apparently killed but, when the emperor approached to inspect the animal, it sprang to its feet and ran off, dragging the emperor behind it after his belts had become entangled in the animal's antlers. It was reported that he was dragged through the forest before a brave servant managed to spring onto the animal's back and cut the belts. Basil was seriously injured, but one of his first acts when the rest of his retinue caught up was to have the servant who had rescued him executed for drawing a knife in the presence of the emperor.

Despite the efforts, the injuries Basil sustained became infected, and he died on August 29, 886 at the age of 74.

Ironically, he was succeeded not by Alexander but by Leo, almost certainly the son of the emperor he had murdered. Rumors, never substantiated, suggested that Basil's death from his injuries was hastened by poison administered by supporters of Leo. Perhaps the most apt summation of Basil's reign was provided by the 11th century historian Psellus who wrote of Basil that he was "more blessed by God than any other family known to me, though rooted in murder and bloodshed."

One of 19-year-old Leo's first acts as Emperor Leo VI was to have the body of Emperor Michael exhumed from an undistinguished grave and reburied in a magnificent new mausoleum in Constantinople. Although no official announcement was ever made, it was assumed by many that this confirmed the fact that Leo's real father was Michael.

A mosaic in the Hagia Sophia depicting Leo

Leo, who became known as Leo the Wise, was an efficient emperor in terms of administering the empire's territories, but he proved much less adept than Basil as a military commander. Under Leo's rule, the Bulgars, former allies, went to war with the empire and took control of large areas of the Balkans. The Muslim Admiral Leo of Tripoli inflicted a series of defeats on the empire and captured the cities of Abydos and Thessaloniki. The city of Constantinople itself was attacked in 907 by Prince Oleg of Kiev, and by the time of Leo's death in 912, the empire was considerably smaller and less powerful than it had been under Basil.

Leo's only legitimate son, Constantine, was just seven-years-old at the time, so Basil's son, Alexander, was appointed as regent. Alexander died in 913, and thereafter, Constantine ruled, initially with the assistance of a series of regents, until 959.

Under his rule, the fortunes of the empire fluctuated. There were some military successes, but also a string of defeats that further reduced the territory controlled by the empire. Part of the problem was that the Byzantine military simply was not large enough to simultaneously fight its Muslim foes and enemies such as the Bulgars in Europe. It was also during this period that the character of the army began to change, with Byzantine troops being supplemented by increasing numbers of foreign mercenaries, including the Varangian Guard.

The origins of the term Varangian are so obscure that they remain difficult to pin down. From the earliest times, Scandinavians, particularly people living in Sweden, carried out raids on the lands of what would become Russia in search of furs and slaves. Gradually, settlements were established to protect trading posts and these became so numerous that Norse writings refer to northern and central parts of Russia as *Svitjod en mikla* ("Great Sweden"). These Swedish settlers referred to themselves as *róðsmenn*, and the local Slavic inhabitants began to refer to them generically as the *Rus*.

The *Rus* established fortified towns across northern and central Russia and gradually came to control an area stretching from Ladoga to Odessa. Intermarriage with the local Slavs led to a gradual loss of their specifically Norse characteristics, and eventually the whole group of people living in that area became known as Russians.

There are several explanations for the term Varangians, which came to be used to describe these Norse inhabitants of Russia. The most widely accepted suggests that the term comes from the Norse word *Vaeringi*, which literally means "companion" but was generally used to denote a Scandinavian who lived as one of the Norse colonists in Russia. In some Russian dialects, the word *Varyaza* is still used to denote a person of foreign origin. From this, the word Varangian arose, usually used to denote a soldier from northern Europe. However, this term was not in use in the early stages of the formation of a foreign Imperial Guard in Constantinople, and the earliest members of this bodyguard of northern European origin were simply referred to as Rus.

As the Rus expanded their territory to the south, they occupied cities such as Kiev and gradually began to encroach on the northernmost territories of the Byzantine Empire. In 860, Rus warriors rampaged through the countryside around Constantinople, though they were unable to take the city itself. After intermittent conflicts over the next 14 years, Basil I was finally able to arrange a peace treaty between the Rus princes and the Byzantine Empire in 874, and one of the clauses of the treaty required that the Rus provide troops for service in the Byzantine army. The emperor was immediately impressed by the size, strength, and fighting ability of these Rus warriors, and it appears that some were integrated into the *Hetaireia*, the Imperial Bodyguard, soon after. The Rus warriors were also impressed, as the Byzantines paid far more than the Rus princes and the conditions in Constantinople were very much to their liking, especially unlimited access to alcohol.

After Basil's death, a series of minor conflicts between the Kievan Rus and the Byzantine Empire broke out. These were finally ended by the signing of the comprehensive and detailed Rus–Byzantine Treaty of 911 by Leo VI. This treaty allowed for Rus merchants to trade within the empire and for the first time specifically mentioned Rus mercenaries serving in the Byzantine army. However, it was not until the reign of another successful Byzantine emperor, Basil II, that these Rus warriors would come to form a distinct and separate unit of Imperial bodyguards.

A medieval depiction of Basil II

Basil II took the throne in 976 following the sudden death of his uncle, Emperor John I Tzimiskes, who had ruled for just seven years but had proved an able military leader, expanding the boundaries of the empire. His sudden death was supposed by some to be the result of poisoning by ambitious generals, and the 21-year-old Basil II became emperor and would rule for almost 50 years.

Despite his long reign, Basil II was never entirely free of the fear of rebellion or even direct attack by his own subordinates. Early in his reign, Basil II faced open rebellion from Bardas Skleros and Bardas Phokas, members of a wealthy elite in Anatolia who resented the power of the empire and in particular the efforts by John to limit the power of major landowners. It was not until 989 that both rebellions were completely suppressed.

One of the things that Basil II had done while fighting these rebellions was to conclude a major treaty with Prince Vladimir I of Kiev. While Basil II was distracted fighting Bardas Skleros and Bardas Phokas, Prince Vladimir had taken the opportunity to attack and occupy the city of Chersonesos, the empire's main base and port in the Crimea. However, Vladimir offered to give the port back to the Byzantine Empire if Basil II was prepared to agree to the marriage of his sister, Anna, to Vladimir. As a further incentive, Vladimir offered to convert to Christianity and to provide 6,000 troops to help Basil II in fighting the rebels. After a great deal of consideration, Basil II agreed. The Rus troops fought valiantly against the rebels, and in 989, Anna married Prince Vladimir in the Crimea. This marked the beginning of a long-term alliance between the Byzantine Empire and the Rus.

It is claimed that the 6,000 troops sent by Prince Vladimir to support Basil II were the most unruly, undisciplined, drunken, and violent men in his army. If so, it seems Vladimir used the obligation to provide troops to Basil II as a way to rid himself of the most troublesome members of his army. However, on the battlefield these men proved to be all but invincible, smashing the enemies of the Byzantine Empire on more than one occasion. At the same time, Basil II remained concerned about the possibility of internal insurrections, so he used these elite troops as his personal bodyguard. They were formally titled the Varangians of the City in 988, replacing the *Exkoubitores* of the *Hetaireia* who had previously guarded the emperor. The Rus troops who served within other Byzantine military and naval units became known as the Varangians Outside the City.

For all these Rus troops, this was a very advantageous move. Suddenly, they were well paid. Members of the Imperial Guard could expect to be paid up to 40 *nomismata* per month, compared to the salary of one *nomismata* per month paid to ordinary members of the provincial army. And of course, those who served as members of the emperor's household had close access to the ultimate seat of power.

Varangians in the Byzantine Army

Since they formed a personal bodyguard for the emperor, the Varangians of the City accompanied Basil II whenever

he left the city of Constantinople on campaign, and given
that the emperor was an active and enthusiastic military
leader who did not seem to enjoy spending time in capital,
the Varangians spent a great deal of time out of the city.
As a result, in addition to guarding the emperor, they took
part in a number of battles. The detailed records of
Byzantine military operations that the empire maintained
do not always make it clear which forces included or were
comprised of Varangians, but the Varangians were
specifically mentioned on occasion, which has allowed
historians to at least partially determine the extent of their
use in the Byzantine military.

During the late 10th century, Basil II led a number of
expeditions against the Fatimid Caliphate, an Ismaili Shia
caliphate that ruled a large part of the Mediterranean coast
of Africa, including Egypt. In October 999, Basil II led a
Byzantine army into present-day Syria to attack Fatimid
forces there. The army besieged the city of Emesa, and the
occupants fled to take refuge in the fortified monastery of
St. Constantine. Byzantine records note that the
Varangians were sent to attack the monastery and set fire
to it, forcing those hiding inside to surrender. The
monastery was then thoroughly plundered, with even the
lead on its roof being taken. This attack failed to destroy
the Fatimid Caliphate, but the caliphate was compelled to

sign a treaty with the Byzantine Empire in 1000 that made it less of a threat.

By the time that treaty was signed, Basil II had already moved his main army to Armenia, where he fought against several rebellious kings and princes. Byzantine historians recorded an incident illustrating that even though the Varangians were an effective fighting force, they were not always completely within the control of the emperor. In Armenia, Basil II called a meeting of local rulers to negotiate a settlement to the conflict, but it seems some Varangians who had been gathering hay for their horses were surprised by the troops of King David, a local ruler of part of northeast Armenia who had been taking part in talks with Basil II. There was a dispute, the Armenian troops tried to take the hay, and at least one Varangian was killed. The whole Varangian contingent in the Byzantine army then attacked the forces of King David. Other Armenian nobles rallied to their comrades' defense, and a pitched battle ensued. The Varangians were victorious, killing not just large numbers of Armenian troops but also a number of princes and military leaders. As many as 30 Armenian and Iberian leaders may have died in the brief battle. There is no record of Basil II's response to this event, but he apparently did not discipline the Varangians for slaughtering large numbers of

Armenians. Moreover, the message was clear that picking a fight with Varangian forces was not a good idea.

After Armenia, Basil II then turned his attention to Bulgaria. There had been ongoing conflicts between the Bulgarian rulers and the Byzantine Empire in the preceding years, and Basil II was determined that there should be one final campaign to end this threat to the empire. From 1001–1014, a series of battles were fought, culminating in the Battle of Kleidion in July 1014 during which the Bulgarian army was completely defeated. 15,000 Bulgarian prisoners were taken, and Basil had 99 men out of every 100 blinded, leaving 1% of the Bulgarians to lead the remainder back to Bulgaria. The ruler of the Bulgarians, King Samuel, was said to have been so distressed at the sight of this blinded army that he suffered a stroke and died within a few days of their arrival home. The war in Bulgaria continued for another four years before all resistance was crushed by 1018, and while it is quite likely the Varangian Guard and other Varangian elements in the Byzantine military took part in this campaign, the records make no specific mention of their activities.

With Bulgaria subdued, Basil returned briefly to Constantinople before beginning yet another campaign in 1021, this time against King Georgi of Georgia. Byzantine military records make specific note of the actions of the

Varangians, particularly their bravery in the final victory at the Battle of Aghpha. The records also make particular note of the extreme brutality of the Varangians. To set an example, Basil II ordered the execution of every man, woman, and child in a number of Georgian provinces. He sent the Varangian forces to do this, and even Byzantine records, which do not generally quail at harsh treatment, described the extreme cruelty of the Varangians in the three months it took them to achieve this.

In the remaining years of his reign, Basil II fought campaigns in Southern Italy and was preparing to lead an invasion of Sicily when he died in December 1025. At the time of his death, the borders of the Byzantine Empire stretched from the Italian peninsula to the Caucasus Mountains, and from the Danube River to the Levant. During his 50 years in power, Basil II made the Byzantine Empire one of the most powerful in the world, and he left the empire in control of more territory than it had ruled for 400 years. He had established the Varangian Guard and placed Varangians in units of the *tagmata* armies and the navy, ensuring they boosted the fighting capabilities of the empire.

Basil II was succeeded by his brother, Constantine VIII Porphyrogenitus, who reigned for just three years before his death in November 1028. He in turn was succeeded by the husband of his daughter Zoe, Romanos III Argyros, who ruled for just six years before his death (or possible murder) in April 1034. Neither Constantine VIII nor Romanos III were capable or enthusiastic military leaders, and there are few records of the activities of the Varangians in the Byzantine army during the reigns of either of these emperors, but it is believed that both retained the Varangian Guard.

The Arrival of Harald Sigurdsson

In 1030, a 15-year-old named Harald Sigurdsson fought in the Battle of Stiklestad alongside his half-brother Olaf Haraldsson. At issue was the throne of Norway, which Olaf had previously occupied before being deposed by Danish King Cnut the Great. After the Norwegians were defeated, Harald and a band of followers were forced into exile, and after this group of Norwegian warriors first went to Kiev before, they came to Constantinople in 1034 to seek employment as part of the Varangian contingent in the Byzantine army.

Harald arrived in Constantinople just as a new emperor had taken the throne. Michael IV the Paphlagonian was the lover of Zoe, wife of the previous emperor Romanos III, and he had been co-emperor before Romanos III's death. It was widely believed that Zoe and Michael murdered Romanos III, either by drowning him in his bath or by poisoning. Zoe and Michael were then immediately married, and Michael was declared emperor with Zoe as his co-emperor. Michael was an astute leader, but he suffered from poor health throughout his life and ruled with the assistance of his brother Constantine.

A medieval depiction of Michael and Zoe's marriage

Harald arrived in Constantinople in the early summer of 1034 with a retinue of around 500 warriors, and historians know a great deal about his period serving the Byzantine Empire not just because it featured largely in the Norse sagas of the kings, but also because Harald was also mentioned in contemporary literature and poetry in England, Iceland, and Denmark. Harald presented himself to the new emperor and offered to serve in the Byzantine army, and for his part, Michael IV seemed happy to accept the service of these admired Norse warriors. Thus, Harald and his men were admitted into the Varangian Guard, despite the fact it was still composed mainly of Kievan Rus soldiers.

However, instead of remaining in Constantinople, Harald and his men were sent to Sicily to fight against Muslim pirates there and elsewhere in the Mediterranean. Harald had no formal appointment as a general in the Byzantine army, but it seems that he was given command of Varangian forces who often fought independently. Harald and his men also fought in campaigns in Sicily and Mesopotamia. Although it is claimed that Harald attempted to keep his royal heritage secret, he rapidly became the acknowledged leader of Varangian forces in the Byzantine army through his ability as a warrior, and when the Byzantine army mounted an expedition to Jerusalem, Harald was at the forefront with the Varangian mercenaries. It is said that Harald and his men were responsible for the capture of 80 Muslim strongholds during these campaigns.

In 1041 a Lombard-Norman revolt against Byzantine rule broke out in southern Italy and Harald and the Varangian Guard were sent to fight for the empire. After the Byzantines were defeated in Italy, Harald and the Varangians were then sent to Bulgaria to fight a rebellion against Byzantine rule led by the "Tzar of Bulgaria," Petar II Delyan. Byzantine forces were victorious there in a campaign that culminated in the Battle of Ostrovo. As before, the Varangians conducted their campaign with great brutality, and after this campaign Harald was given the nickname *Bolgara brennir* ("Bulgar burner") by his followers.

Harald was promoted to the role of *manglabites*, a senior rank in the Imperial Guard, following the campaign in Sicily, and then to *spatharokandidatos*, the third-highest rank in the Byzantine military, following his victory in Bulgaria. However, Harald's favorable position in the Byzantine court was undermined by the death of Emperor Michael IV. Although Zoe was co-emperor, Michael clearly did not trust his wife, perhaps because of her involvement in the murder of his predecessor. Michael had Zoe confined to the women's quarters of the Imperial Palace and kept her out of any role of power in the empire. Michael became increasingly ill and in December he died, refusing to see his wife before his demise. He was succeeded as emperor by his nephew, Michael V.

Within a few months of taking power, Michael V banished his co-emperor Zoe to the island of Principo in the Marmara Sea on charges of attempting to poison him. When this became known in Constantinople, it caused a popular revolt, and when the Imperial Palace was surrounded by a mob, Michael was forced to flee. In April, just five months after his coronation, he was arrested, castrated, blinded, and imprisoned. Michael was succeeded as emperor by Zoe, initially with her sister Theodora as co-emperor. Theodora was replaced after

Zoe's marriage to a former lover, Constantine IX, who became co-emperor with her.

During this turmoil, things did not go well for Harald and the Varangians. During the brief reign of Michael V, the Varangians were replaced as the emperor's personal bodyguards by Scythians known to the emperor, and Harald and two other Varangian leaders were arrested and imprisoned on a charge of withholding money from the emperor. There is some doubt about whether there was any truth in this charge because Michael V clearly did not entirely trust the Varangians and may have sought a convenient way to reduce Harald's growing power. It was certainly true that Harald had become very wealthy as a result of plunder taken during the campaigns that he and the Varangians had taken part in, and it seems that the rumor that he was keeping more than his due originated with Zoe. What is known is that Harald was released from prison just at the time that a mob was surrounding the Imperial Palace, and it was Varangians led by Harald who entered the palace and castrated and blinded the emperor.

When Zoe became emperor, Harald asked to be allowed to leave Byzantine service and return to Kievan Rus with his men. This was refused, but, in late 1042, Harald escaped and was able to travel back to Kiev. Shortly after his arrival there, the ruler of Kiev, Yaroslav the Wise, mounted an unsuccessful attack on the city of

Constantinople. It was assumed that Harald had provided information to give this the best chance of success.

In 1046, Harald returned to Scandinavia and, with the wealth amassed during his service in the Byzantine Empire, raised an army with which he was able to take the throne of Norway. He ruled as Norway's king for 20 years, and during his reign he acquired the epithet *Hardrada* ("hard ruler"). He would personally lead an invasion of England that culminated in his death at the Battle of Stamford Bridge in 1066, an event that contributed directly to the victory of William of Normandy at the Battle of Hastings a short time later.

The Komnenian Restoration

Despite the escape of Harald and his followers, the Varangians, and in particular the Varangian Guard, remained a significant and respected part of the Byzantine forces. Many accounts of the reign of Empress Zoe mention her being accompanied by "the men who carry axes on their right shoulders," a clear reference to the Varangian Guard.

Under Zoe and Constantine IX, the empire was forced to fight several campaigns to maintain the borders of the empire, and by the autumn of 1047, the only troops left in the capital were mercenaries, including the Varangian Guard. Sensing an opportunity, a general from a noble

Byzantine family, Leo Tornicius, led a revolt and laid siege to Constantinople. The only thing standing between the Byzantine rulers and disaster were the mercenary troops of the Imperial Guard. The Varangians proved to be loyal to Zoe and Constantine IX and helped defeat the uprising, which ended with the execution of Leo Tornicius.

A mosaic depicting Constantine IX

In 1048, the ongoing conflict with the Seljuk Turks flared back up when the semi-nomadic Pechenegs launched an invasion of Bulgaria. The Varangians took part in the campaign against the Pechenegs, and their contributions included attacking a band of marauding Pecheneg warriors near the city of Constantinople. All the Pechenegs were killed in the battle that followed, and the Varangians brought the heads of the dead back to the city and laid them at the feet of the emperor. The Varangians, under their new commander *Akoluthos* Michael, also defeated the Pechenegs in two major battles and forced them to reach a 30-year truce with the empire.

After Constantine IX died in January 1055, the Byzantine Empire entered a period of turmoil. Constantine IX was succeeded by Theodora, the only surviving member of the royal family, but she died in August 1056 after ruling for just 18 months. She in turn was succeeded by an elderly member of the court, Michael VI Bringas, and almost as soon as he became emperor, Michael VI had to deal with a conspiracy led by Theodosios, the nephew of Constantine IX. The Varangians were involved in suppressing the uprising and executing Theodosios, but even after that revolt was put down, Michael VI was never able to count on the support of the leaders of the Byzantine army. Rebellions continued, and there were ongoing battles between supporters of Constantine IX and supporters of a prominent military leader, Isaac Komnenos, a general who had served with distinction under several emperors since Basil II. Varangians fought on both sides of what turned into a civil war, and there were even instances where Varangian units fought against one another. In August 1057, Isaac Komnenos was crowned Emperor Isaac I Komnenos.

The internal conflict that led to Isaac I becoming emperor required Byzantine troops to be removed from border areas, and the provincial army was also smaller at this time, partly because Constantine IX had agreed that Armenian provinces would no longer be required to provide troops for the thematic army. Instead, the Armenian provinces were required to make annual payments into the Imperial treasury, which made sense because one of Constantine IX's main aims had been to balance the books and to restore the depleted treasury. However, this left the provincial army dangerously small, especially due to the increasing Turkish threat, and it meant that the Byzantine army was even more reliant on foreign mercenaries.

Despite the fact that some of them had fought against him, Isaac I regarded the Varangians highly, and all of them were integrated into the reformed Byzantine army and the Varangian Guard. Emperor Isaac undertook only one military campaign, against the Hungarians and resurgent Pechenegs in the summer of 1059, and

Varangian troops were involved in several successful battles.

Ill health forced Isaac I to abdicate in 1059 in favor of Constantine X Doukas, who had been a part of the Byzantine Civil Service and, like Constantine IX, aimed to reduce the debt. He saved money in part through withholding payments to military units, though not to the Varangian Guard, which he needed to assure his own safety. He also raised taxes, making him unpopular with the general population. Perhaps unsurprisingly, there were several attempts to assassinate this emperor, but none were successful. Constantine X did not lead any military campaigns, but in 1066 he did send an army comprising mainly Varangian troops to the port city of Bari in an attempt to conquer the Italian peninsula for the empire.

The battles in Italy continued for five years until all Byzantine forces there were finally defeated and the empire lost all control over Italy in 1071. Part of the harbor at Bari is still known as *Mare dei Guaranghi* ("Varangian Sea").

By the time Italy was lost, the empire had a new ruler, Romanos IV Diogenes, who was determined to reverse the decline of the Byzantine army and increased military expenditures, particularly on foreign mercenaries. Romanos IV led several campaigns against Turkish forces, but he was captured after a disastrous defeat at the Battle of Manzikert in 1071. While he was being held captive, there was a coup in Constantinople, and he was replaced by Michael VII Doukas.

Despite yet another change in ruler, the Varangian Guard continued to function as the emperor's personal bodyguard, and Varangian troops continued to play an important role in the Byzantine army and navy. However, discipline in the army, particularly in non-Varangian foreign units, declined rapidly at the same time, and on more than one occasion the Varangians were used to fight marauding bands of mercenaries who had defected to fight against the empire. The situation with rebelling mercenaries became so serious that Michael VII was forced to make a treaty with the Seljuk Turks in order to free up loyal forces to fight against the mercenaries. He was eventually successful in this, but the expenditures on military forces became too much to sustain, to the point that even the Varangians stopped receiving payments. They subsequently joined a rebellion that removed Michael from the throne and had him replaced with a former Byzantine army general, Nikephoros III Botaneiates, in 1078.

The new emperor was beset by problems from the beginning and these were made much worse when the Norman Duke Robert Guiscard of Apulia prepared to invade the Byzantine Empire. Nikephoros III appointed a Byzantine general, Alexios Komnenos to lead an army to confront the Norman invaders, but Alexios instead used the army to mount a rebellion and sacked the city of Constantinople. Nikephoros was forced to abdicate, and Alexios I Komnenos was crowned the new emperor in April 1081.

A contemporary portrait of Alexios I Komnenos

After the coronation of Alexios I, the Byzantine Empire finally found the stability it so desperately needed. The empire had endured 12 emperors in a period of little more than 50 years, most of whom were removed by plots, murder, or open rebellion, and the empire was close to collapse. Alexios I would rule for 37 years and would begin a resurgence in the empire's fortunes that has become known as the Komnenian restoration. For the next 100 years, the empire would be ruled by just three emperors and enjoy a stable succession, and throughout this period the Varangians would remain an important part of the army.

Under the rule of Alexios I, the Byzantine Empire, and the role of Varangians within it, changed dramatically. Most notably, Alexios I began to seek assistance from other European states to fight against Muslim incursions, leading to the Crusades. Meanwhile, the traditional supply routes between Kiev and Constantinople gradually fell into disuse and the supply of Rus mercenaries also declined. Later, the Kievan Rus state broke up into several competing principalities and the supply of Rus warriors available for hire effectively ended. As a result, the Varangian Guard and other Varangian units in the Byzantine army began recruiting soldiers from other ethnic backgrounds.

The presence of Danes in Varangian units was first mentioned during the operations around the Italian city of Bari in 1066, and when Alexios I mounted a campaign against the city of Antioch in 1098, the participation of Danish troops is specifically mentioned. During one of the first Crusades, in 1102, the Danish King Eric I the Good visited Constantinople, and the contemporary records indicate the king was welcomed by the Danes serving in the Varangian Guard. In 1195, Byzantine Emperor Isaac II Angelos sent an envoy to the Danish king specifically requesting 1,000 soldiers to serve as mercenaries, and in 1203, Danish troops defended the cities of Blachernae and Galata from Venetian attacks.

After the Norman conquest of England in 1066, increasing numbers of Anglo-Saxon mercenaries began to arrive in Constantinople, and many joined Varangian units. In fact, within 200 years, English troops would form the majority of these units, and English would become the language spoken by Varangians in Byzantine service.

The first mention of English mercenaries in Varangian forces comes from an account of the Battle of Dyrrhachium, which explained that Varangian forces under the command of Alexios I included English troops. The emperor was so happy with the performance of these troops in battle that he granted them lands around the city of Kivit (near Nicomedia) and called them to serve in the army and bodyguard as required. In contemporary records, it was said that over 4,000 Anglo-Saxons settled in Kivit and Constantinople, and many more were said to have occupied lands, with the emperor's permission, in the north near the Black Sea. They named this area New

England and gave the towns there English names in memory of their lost homeland.

  The influx of Anglo-Saxons into the Byzantine Empire certainly meant that Varangian units recruited more of these troops, but there is some debate regarding precise numbers. It is notable that during the rule of Alexios I, the terms for "Varangian" and "Englishman" were used interchangeably, and by the end of the 11th century, Byzantine records mention English members of the Varangian Guard and other Varangian units far more frequently than any other nationality.

  While the numbers of Anglo-Saxon Varangians certainly increased dramatically following the Norman invasion, mercenaries also started to arrive from other Nordic countries. Norwegians and Swedes had always been part of Varangian units, and their numbers increased during the era of Harald Sigurdsson. However, it seems that there were also large numbers of Icelanders present in Varangian units - one Byzantine record described the appointment of an Icelandic warrior known as "Coalbeard" as commander of the Varangian Guard at the beginning of the 11th century. Moreover, Bolli Bollason, one of the main characters in the epic Icelandic saga *The Saga of the People of Laxardal,* served with a number of his followers in the Varangian Guard.

Byzantine records and other sources also listed Nordic warriors from the island of "Tula," "Thule," or "Tul" who served bravely in Varangian units, and there is some debate about these soldiers. Historians have variously interpreted this as meaning Norway, Iceland, or even Britain.

Though the ethnic background of these units may have changed, their abilities and effectiveness in combat definitely did not. When he had established himself as emperor, Alexios I first turned his attention to defeating the threatened Norman invasion. At the Battle of Dyrrhachium in 1081, Varangians fought on the left wing of the Byzantine army and drove back the right wing of the opposing Norman army. The war against the Normans ended with Duke Guiscard's death in 1085, and Alexios I was able to recapture all the territory in the Balkans that the Normans had occupied.

Throughout the reign of Alexios I, the emperor led a number of campaigns against the Seljuk Turks and the Serbs. These campaigns secured and expanded the borders of the empire, and while the Varangians don't appear by name in any of the records, they almost certainly were involved.

When Alexios I died in August 1118, he was succeeded by his eldest son, John II Komnenos, and during his 25-

five-year reign, John II became revered as the greatest Byzantine emperor since Justinian the Great. He was an astute military commander who favored siege operations over open battle whenever possible, and he led successful campaigns against the Pechenegs, the Hungarians and the Serbs in the Balkans while also driving back Turkish forces. Under John II's rule, the borders of the Byzantine Empire extended across the Anatolian peninsula and into southern Turkey, an expansion that left the Byzantines in charge of over 10 million subjects.

A mosaic of John II in the Hagia Sophia

Once again, it seems certain that John II used Varangian forces in his military operations, though there are few specific references in contemporary records. It was noted that the decisive victory against the Pechenegs at the Battle of Beroia in 1122 was achieved in part due to the bravery and fighting prowess of the "axe-bearers," a clear reference to Varangian units.

In April 1142, while preparing for an assault on the city of Antioch, John II decided to go wild boar hunting, and during the hunt, he accidentally cut himself with a poisoned arrow and died a few days later. Before his death, he named Manuel, the younger of his sons, to be his successor, so Manuel I Komnenos was crowned as Byzantine emperor on April 8, 1143. He would rule for 37 years, and though he attempted to continue the revival started by the previous two emperors, he had mixed success.

A mosaic of Manuel I

The Varangians took part in a number of operations during the rule of Manuel I, and there is more information about their participation during this time. For example, when a Byzantine army besieged the Norman-occupied city of Thebes early in 1149, the Byzantine commander, Stephen Contostephanus, was killed. After his death, "the commander of the axe-bearers" was put in charge of the army, the Normans were quickly defeated, and the city was taken.

In 1154, the emperor's cousin, Andronicus, attempted to have the emperor assassinated and have himself established as emperor. First, Andronicus attempted to kill the emperor himself when he was sleeping in a tent, but he was foiled by members of the Varangian Guard. Next, Andronicus persuaded a troop of Isaurians to ambush and murder the emperor, but before this could be done, the plot was discovered and Isaac, commander of the Varangian Guard, was able to arrest Andronicus.

In 1155, Prince Renault de Châtillon of Antioch attacked the Byzantine-controlled island of Cyprus, defended by a garrison of Varangians in the city of Paphos. After a series of battles that lasted almost an entire year, de Chatillon was defeated, captured, and brought to Constantinople by the Varangians.

The End of the Byzantine Empire

In 1175, Manuel I personally led yet another campaign against the Seljuk Turks, and he brought with him not just the Varangian Guard, but several Varangian units of the *tagmata* army as part of an army totaling nearly 35,000. The Turks, alarmed by the size of the approaching army, offered to make peace on generous terms, but Manuel refused, believing that he could finally crush the Turkish threat forever.

Instead, Manuel led his army into one of the most disastrous defeats in Byzantine history. While marching through a narrow mountain pass in the Highlands of Anatolia in September 1176, the Byzantine army was ambushed by forces commanded by Seljuk Sultan Kilij Arslan II at what would become known as the Battle of Myriokephalon. Trapped in the narrow pass, the vast Byzantine army was unable to maneuver and was destroyed in piecemeal fashion by the attacking Turks. Manuel himself was severely wounded, and virtually all members of the Varangian Guard were killed. Manuel was able to escape with the tattered remnants of his army, but the power of the Byzantine Empire and the aura of invincibility that surrounded the Varangians was irrevocably diminished.

After the Battle of Myriokephalon, the Byzantine Empire was forced to make peace with the Turks and withdraw from forts and towns that they had previously occupied. A year later, in 1177, a large Seljuk Turk army advanced into Byzantine territory and was comprehensively defeated at the Battle of Hyelion and Leimocheir, but in 1179, another Turkish army laid siege to the Byzantine city of Claudiopolis in Bithynia. Manuel led a force of cavalry that included Varangians to relieve the siege and drive the Turks back.

In time, the continuous campaigns and the shock of the defeat at Myriokephalon affected Manuel's vitality and then his health. He became ill with a slow fever and died in September 1180, marking the end of the Komnenian restoration and the start of the empire's gradual decline.

Manuel was succeeded by his son, Alexius II, who was just 12, so his mother, the Dowager Empress Marie, acted as regent on his behalf. She quickly had to deal with a revolt led by supporters of Maria, Manuel I's daughter by his first marriage. With the support of the Varangians this attempted uprising was crushed, but soon after another rebellion arose. This one was led by Andronicus, the man who had tried to have Manuel I assassinated but had been thwarted by the Varangians. It is difficult for historians to ascertain exactly what happened, but it seems that the Varangians may have supported Andronicus and may even have helped to seize the young emperor. Alexius II was blinded and imprisoned, Maria was killed, and Andronicus had himself crowned emperor Andronicus I Komnenos in September 1183.

Andronicus I quickly proved himself to be a brutal ruler who distrusted foreigners and those who did not belong to the Orthodox Church. He instituted the Massacre of the Latins, which led to the deaths of thousands of Roman

Catholics and large numbers of people from the West, in April 1182. He also implemented a number of measures to curb the power of feudal landowners, the people who were behind the provincial army.

It does not appear that Andronicus I trusted or was trusted by the Varangian Guard, a crucial mistake for an unpopular emperor who needed his personal bodyguard to assure his safety. In September 1185, Andronicus I left the city of Constantinople to visit other locations in the empire, and while he was absent, a Byzantine military leader, Isaac Angelos, staged a coup without opposition from the Varangians and had himself declared Emperor Isaac II Angelos. When Andronicus returned to the city, he was handed over to an enraged mob who literally tore him apart.

Isaac II proved an ineffective military leader who was unable to stop the advance of Seljuk Turks into Byzantine territory. Although the Byzantine records are silent about the Varangians' actions during his reign, they must have been involved in the many battles that took place as the once mighty empire began to fragment. A lack of money in the treasury forced Isaac II to cut back on military spending, and the Byzantine navy, once one of the most powerful in the Mediterranean, had dwindled to just 30 ships by 1195. The lack of funds likely applied to the hiring of foreign mercenaries for the army and perhaps even for the Varangian Guard.

In April 1195, the emperor left the city of Constantinople to take part in a hunting trip, and while he was absent, his older brother, Alexios Angelos, staged a coup and had himself crowned Emperor Alexios III Angelos. When Isaac returned to the city, he was blinded and imprisoned. Given what happened, the Varangian Guard presumably made no attempt to prevent this coup or protect the former emperor.

One of the first acts of the new emperor was to send messages to the kings of Sweden, Denmark, and Norway requesting additional troops for the Varangian Guard. He clearly understood the necessity of having a bodyguard loyal to him alone, and while some Scandinavians did come to Constantinople to join the Varangian Guard, the numbers that arrived were far fewer than they would have been in previous centuries. It was obvious that the Byzantine Empire was tottering. Alexios III reigned for eight years, and the Varangian Guard spent much of that time quelling riots and insurrection in the capital rather than fighting the empire's foreign enemies. On at least one occasion, only the Varangian Guard stood between the emperor and a rioting mob intent on murdering him.

The end of Alexios III's reign and the effective end of the Varangian Guard came in 1202, one of the most notorious years in the history of Christianity. That year, a crusade of Western Christians, or Franks, as the Byzantines would have called them, set out to conquer Egypt from the Saracens. The Republic of Venice agreed to transport the crusaders for a considerable sum, and when they proved themselves unable or unwilling to provide payment, the Doge of Venice found that he had some 12,000 troops on his doorstep, fully armed and frustrated. The doge agreed to transport the crusaders to Egypt if they would take the tiny Christian city of Zara on the Dalmatian coast. This they did, for which Pope Innocent III excommunicated the crusaders and forbade them to attack any more Christian communities.

In the wake of that fiasco, Alexios Angelos, the son of the deposed and blinded Isaac II, traveled to Venice and persuaded the crusaders to attack the city of Constantinople, depose Alexios, and restore Isaac as emperor. The crusaders' zeal for gold overpowered their zeal for religion, and they agreed. The old and blind Doge of Venice, Enrico Dandolo (1107-1205), who could not overlook the chance of enriching himself and Venice, also joined the venture.

The crusaders landed near Constantinople in June 1203, at a time when the Byzantine navy comprised no more than 20 outdated ships. The garrison in Constantinople was normally quite modest in size, so when the Franks approached the city, there were only 15,000 men there. Normally when the city was threatened, troops from the provinces would be called in, but at this time the attack was so sudden and unexpected that there was no time for these troops to arrive. Alexios III's troops outnumbered the crusaders considerably, but the emperor's courage failed and he fled his troops. The inhabitants of Constantinople then recalled Isaac II to the throne, thus depriving Prince Alexios Angelos of any claim to the throne and the crusaders of a pretext to attack the city. Isaac made his son co-emperor, and with the crown finally upon his head, the Franks demanded their reward.

Unsurprisingly, Alexis IV found it impossible to give the crusaders the vast amounts of money he had promised them. Fighting broke out between the impatient crusaders and the citizens of Constantinople. Then Isaac II died and the population, sickened by the incompetent Alexis IV, who raided the sacred sites of the city to raise money to placate the hated Franks, deposed him and chose a young nobleman by the name of Alexis Doukas, who became Alexis V. Alexios IV and his father were seized and imprisoned. Isaac died of shock while his son was strangled in February 1204.

With the overwhelming support of the people, the new emperor vowed to remove the hated Franks from sacred soil. He called in troops from the provinces and the crusaders felt compelled to act. Despite explicit instructions from the Pope to the contrary, the crusaders resolved to take the city and recover what they felt was owed them. On April 12, 1204, they breached the walls of Constantinople and by the end of the following day had slaughtered its defenders and begun to sack the city. For three days, the soldiers of God looted, murdered, raped, and maimed, all of which led the Greeks across the empire to demonize the Westerners for centuries.

During the crusaders' sack of Constantinople, the Varangians refused to fight since they had not been paid. By the end of it, the Varangian Guard surrendered. When the churches of the city had no more treasures to plunder, the crusaders elected one of their leaders, Baldwin of Flanders, as the first emperor of the Latin Empire. The Byzantines continued to rule in three successor states: the Empire of Nicaea in western Asia Minor, where Theodore I Lascaris, son-in-law of Alexios III, had fled; the Empire of Trebizond on the Black Sea's coast; and the Depostate of Epirus covering the area of modern Albania and northwestern Greece.

In 1261, Emperor Michael VIII Palaeologus of Nicaea recaptured Constantinople, but the empire never recovered from the fall of the city in 1204. In the east, a new threat, the Ottoman Turks, pillaged imperial lands and pushed the Byzantines back to the Aegean Sea. In Europe, the

Western powers established a permanent presence and habitually interfered in Byzantine affairs, especially the trading republics of Venice and Genoa. Moreover, in the Balkans, the states of Serbia and Bulgaria experienced a resurgence and threatened the integrity of the empire in Europe.

In order to maintain the army and the navy, the population of the empire had to be heavily taxed. This made the government so unpopular that Emperor Andronicus II (r. 1282-1328) drastically reduced the military in order to relieve the people and avoid an insurrection. The powerful cataphracts and infantry phalanxes were replaced by light infantry and cavalry.

By 1320 the emperor could maintain no more than 4,000 men, often hastily conscripted and poorly trained. This came just as the Ottomans began invading Europe, further depriving the empire of resources and manpower. By 1453, the once mighty Byzantine Empire had been reduced to little more than the city of Constantinople itself. The city possessed a garrison of only 1,500, and a great proportion of these were foreign troops. The vast fortifications of Constantinople and its environs became increasingly expensive to maintain and garrison, though the city walls were in good shape when the Ottomans launched their final attack.

Mercenaries had always been under the control of the emperor, but mercenaries hired in the declining years of the Byzantine Empire were conscious of the ability to exercise political power over their employers. The most notorious of these opportunists were the elite warriors of the Catalan Company, led by Roger de Flor. In 1303, Emperor Andronicus II paid Roger and his men to repel the Ottoman invasion in Asia Minor, a task which he would have probably accomplished had not Byzantine politics intervened. Roger sought to make himself leader of the empire, an ambition that led both to the destruction of the Company and the further debilitation of the Empire.

In the final years of the Byzantine Empire, Constantine XI (r. 1449-1453) desperately sought assistance from the West, obtaining a little help in the form of a few soldiers on humiliating terms. The emperor was obliged to submit the Orthodox Church to the jurisdiction of the Pope, an action which his subjects, remembering the 1204 sack of Constantinople, utterly ignored.

In 1453, as the Ottoman Turks prepared to attack Constantinople, Constantine made an assessment of the city's sorry defenses. The city which had once claimed to rule the civilized world could now call just 7,000 able-bodied men to the city walls.[9] These included 2,000 foreigners, most of whom were Genoese and Venetians.

---

[9] Freely, John, *Istanbul: the Imperial City*, Penguin Books London 1998, p173

The Ottomans challenged this tiny force with an army of 80,000 men.

By then, the Varangian Guard was nothing more than a distant memory, and by the end of the year, the Byzantine Empire would cease to exist.

Conclusion

For over two hundred years the Varangian Guard was a conspicuous and crucial staple of the Byzantine Empire. Emperors may have come and gone, but all of them recognized the value of a personal bodyguard that stood apart from the intrigues of the court. Furthermore, their fighting capabilities were so renowned that large numbers of Varangians fought within the *tagmata* army and the navy.

While the Varangians played important roles in important battles, the Varangian Guard became and remained famous for being the emperor's personal bodyguard. A contingent of the Varangian Guard accompanied the emperor wherever he or she went in the city, and one Byzantine record pointed out that even when the emperor attended church, he was preceded by a group of the Varangian Guard who would stand behind the seat that the emperor would take, axes in hand. When the emperor arrived, they would shoulder their axes and scan the congregation for potential threats. The Varangian

Guard was also responsible for guarding important political prisoners, torturing prisoners to extract information, and for carrying out punishments such as blinding or the amputation of limbs. Inevitably, they also took part in executions.

Throughout their existence, the Varangians required and maintained strict discipline, and any judgments and punishments meted out against Varangians were passed down by senior members of the Varangian Guard themselves. One famous story recounted that when a member of the Varangian Guard attempted to rape a local woman and she killed him in self-defense, other members of the Varangian Guard went to her home and gave her all the property belonging to the man who had tried to rape her.

A medieval depiction of a woman killing a Varangian

The main weapon used by all Varangian units, including the Varangian Guard, was the axe. This was a common and fearsome weapon amongst Norse warriors but the Varangians, who are often referred to in contemporary records as the "axe-bearers," seem to have been the only element of the Byzantine army to have used this weapon. Contemporary illustrations show a single-edged axe with a spear-point above the blade, but many historians have suggested that this is artistic license, and that the Varangian axe would most likely have been a large double-edged weapon which could be used effectively only by tall, strong soldiers.

The unique weapon was emblematic of the many ways the Varangians remained quite separate from the rest of the Byzantine army and the court. They spoke their own language, initially Rus and then English, and they communicated with the emperor and his entourage through interpreters. This seems to have been part of a deliberate policy of keeping the Varangians apart from possible plots or intrigues and ensure that they remained directly loyal only to the emperor or empress.

Though the Varangian Guard ceased to exist over 800 years ago, the actions of these fearsome warriors passed into legend thanks to the accounts in Byzantium and through sagas and folk tales in the lands from which they came. While those tales are impressive in their own right, nothing speaks to the impact and impression the Varangians left than the fact that even as the Byzantine

Empire's military and its accomplishments are largely forgotten today, the mercenaries who comprised the Varangian Guard are the empire's most famous soldiers.

Online Resources

Other books about medieval history by Charles River Editors

Other books about the Byzantines on Amazon

Further Reading

Ball, Warwick (2016). Rome in the East: Transformation of an Empire, 2nd edition. London & New York: Routledge, ISBN 978-0-415-72078-6.

Bury, J. B. (1958). History of the Later Roman Empire: From the Death of Theodosius I to the Death of Justinian. Dover Publications.

Crowley, Roger (2005). Constantinople: Their Last Great Siege, 1453. Faber and Faber. ISBN 978-0-571-22185-1.

Freely, John (1998). Istanbul: The Imperial City. Penguin. ISBN 978-0-14-024461-8.

Freely, John; Ahmet S. Cakmak (2004). The Byzantine Monuments of Istanbul. Cambridge University Press. ISBN 978-0-521-77257-0.

Gibbon, Edward (2005). The Decline and Fall of the Roman Empire. Phoenix Press. ISBN 978-0-7538-1881-7.

Hanna-Riitta, Toivanen (2007). The Influence of Constantinople on Middle Byzantine Architecture (843–1204). A typological and morphological approach at the provincial level. Suomen kirkkohistoriallisen seuran toimituksia 202 (Publications of the Finnish Society of Church History No. 202). ISBN 978-952-5031-41-6.

Harris, Jonathan. Constantinople: Capital of Byzantium. Bloomsbury, 2nd edition, 2017. ISBN 978-1-4742-5465-6.

Harris, Jonathan. Byzantium and the Crusades. Bloomsbury, 2nd edition, 2014. ISBN 978-1-78093-767-0.

Herrin, Judith (2008). Byzantium: The Surprising Life of a Medieval Empire. Princeton University Press. ISBN 978-0-691-13151-1.

Hirth, Friedrich (2000) [1885]. Jerome S. Arkenberg, ed. "East Asian History Sourcebook: Chinese Accounts of Rome, Byzantium and the Middle East, c. 91 B.C.E. – 1643 C.E." Fordham.edu. Fordham University. Retrieved 2016-09-10.

Janin, Raymond (1964). Constantinople Byzantine (in French) (2 ed.). Paris: Institut Français d'Etudes Byzantines.

Korolija Fontana-Giusti, Gordana 'The Urban Language of Early Constantinople: The Changing Roles of the Arts and Architecture in the Formation of the New Capital and the New Consciousness' in Intercultural Transmission in the Medieval Mediterranean, (2012), Stephanie L. Hathaway and David W. Kim (eds), London: Continuum, pp 164–202. ISBN 978-1-4411-3908-5.

Mamboury, Ernest (1953). The Tourists' Istanbul. Istanbul: Çituri Biraderler Basımevi.

Mansel, Philip (1998). Constantinople: City of the World's Desire, 1453–1924. St. Martin's Griffin. ISBN 978-0-312-18708-8.

Meyendorff, John (1996). Rome, Constantinople, Moscow: Historical and Theological Studies. Crestwood, NY: St. Vladimir's Seminary Press. ISBN 9780881411348.

Müller-Wiener, Wolfgang (1977). Bildlexikon zur Topographie Istanbuls: Byzantion, Konstantinupolis, Istanbul bis zum Beginn d. 17 Jh (in German). Tübingen: Wasmuth. ISBN 978-3-8030-1022-3.

Phillips, Jonathan (2005). The Fourth Crusade and the Sack of Constantinople. Pimlico. ISBN 978-1-84413-080-1.

Runciman, Steven (1990). The Fall of Constantinople, 1453. Cambridge University Press. ISBN 978-1-84413-080-1.

Treadgold, Warren (1997). A History of the Byzantine State and Society. Stanford University Press. ISBN 978-0-8047-2630-6.

Yule, Henry (1915). Henri Cordier (ed.), Cathay and the Way Thither: Being a Collection of Medieval Notices of China, Vol I: Preliminary Essay on the Intercourse Between China and the Western Nations Previous to the Discovery of the Cape Route. London: Hakluyt Society. Accessed 21 September 2016.

Evans, Helen C.; Wixom, William D (1997). The glory of Byzantium: art and culture of the Middle Byzantine era, A.D. 843–1261. New York: The Metropolitan Museum of Art. ISBN 978-0-8109-6507-2. Retrieved 2016-02-19.

Bogdanović, Jelena (2016). The Relational Spiritual Geopolitics of Constantinople, the Capital of the Byzantine Empire. Boulder : University Press of Colorado.

Free Books by Charles River Editors

We have brand new titles available for free most days of the week. To see which of our titles are currently free, click on this link.

Discounted Books by Charles River Editors

We have titles at a discount price of just 99 cents everyday. To see which of our titles are currently 99 cents, click on this link.